Original idea and texts
Lorenzo Domizioli, M.Cristina Zannoner, Paola Pacetti (pp.26-30)

Specialist consultant on texts
Diletta Corsini

Illustrations
Manuela Cappon

Cartoon illustrations
Roberto Luciani

Graphic design
Rocío Isabel González

Picture research
Cristina Reggioli,
Morgana Clinto

Photographic research
Archivio Giunti
Archivio Giunti /Rabatti-Domingie, Florence
Archivio Giunti / Marcello Bertoni, Florence
Nicolò Orsi Battaglini, Florence
Rabatti-Domingie, Florence
Atlantide, Florence
Mairani / Grazia Neri, Milan
Paolo Bacherini, Florence
Massimo Listri / Corbis / Grazia Neri, Milan
Special thanks to:
Cassa di Risparmio di Firenze / Foto Liberto Perugi
Museo Stibbert, Florence
Museo dei Ragazzi, Florence

Translation
Jeremy Carden for n.t.l., Florence

ISBN 88-09-02018-9

© 2001 Giunti Gruppo Editoriale, Florence
First edition: January 2001

Reprinted	Year
6 5 4 3 2 1 0	2005 2004 2003 2002 2001

Printed in the Giunti Industrie Grafiche S.p.A. printing works in Prato

FLORENCE

a young
travellers'
guide

GIUNTI

contents

contents

FLORENCE

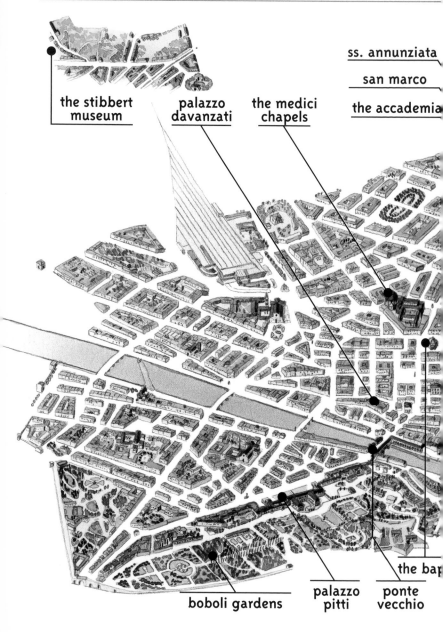

the stibbert museum

palazzo davanzati

the medici chapels

ss. annunziata

san marco

the accademia

the bap

boboli gardens

palazzo pitti

ponte vecchio

8

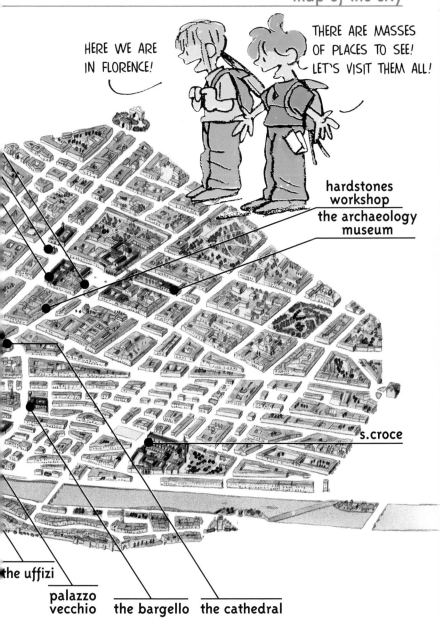

HERE WE ARE IN FLORENCE!

THERE ARE MASSES OF PLACES TO SEE! LET'S VISIT THEM ALL!

hardstones workshop

the archaeology museum

s.croce

the uffizi

palazzo vecchio   the bargello   the cathedral

9

The **lantern of the dome**. It's called the lantern because it lets the light in. You can climb up it.

The **dome** is made up of segments, 8 in all.

You can climb up Giotto's bell-tower as well. It's not quite as high as the dome.

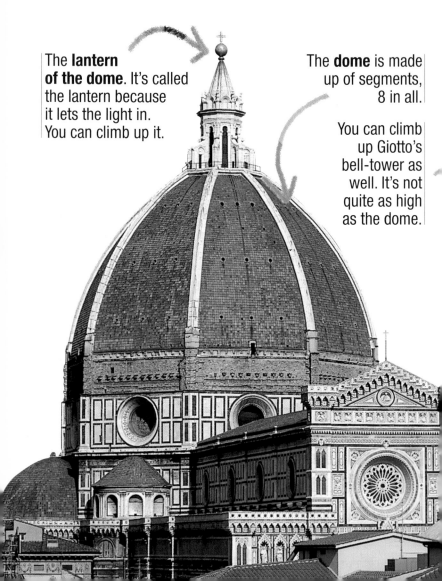

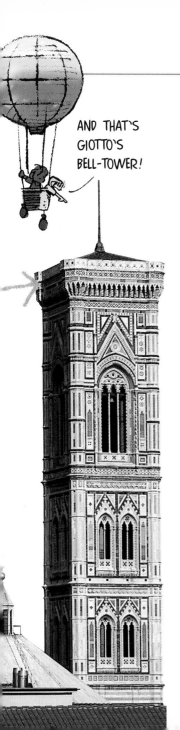

AND THAT'S GIOTTO'S BELL-TOWER!

The dome is an engineering miracle because while it was being built it held itself up without the help of scaffolding. The credit for this must go to the architect Filippo Brunelleschi. The white stripes you can see are called ribs because they can be thought of as the ribs of the structure. The segments between one rib and another look like wind-filled sails and in fact they're known as 'sails'. The red tiles and white marble are visible from a long way away, and it's partly thanks to the dome that the cathedral – its full name is Santa Maria del Fiore – was for a long time the biggest church in the world. Now it's in fourth place!

Actually there are two domes, one inside and one outside. They're like two skins held together by the ribs.
In the space between them there are 463 steps going all the way to the top.

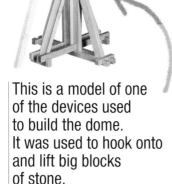

This is a model of one of the devices used to build the dome.
It was used to hook onto and lift big blocks of stone.

All round the dome there are animals and monsters looking down. You can't see them from the ground but the medieval artists sculpted them for the 'eye of God', which can see everything.
These little monsters also have a practical use: the rain water that falls onto the dome flows away through their open mouths.

This enormous fresco of the **Final Judgement** covers the inside of the dome. It's so high you can't see all the details from the ground, but if you climb into the gallery at the base you get a better view of the angels, the saints, the prophets… and of course the horrible faces of the devils.

In front of the cathedral
is the **baptistery**.
It's a small eight-sided
church and was used
to baptise children.

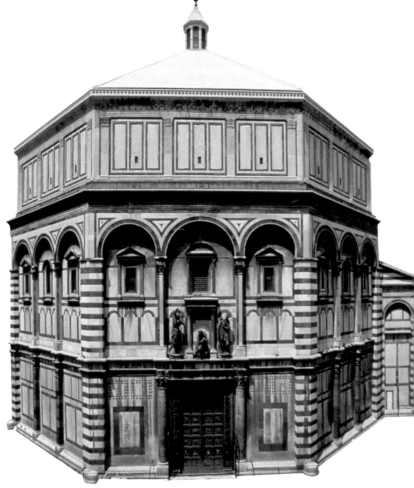

18

One of the three sets of bronze doors of the baptistery is called the **'gates of paradise'**. It's a kind of illustrated Bible, and the eight picture stories enabled those who couldn't read to understand as well.

One of the stories carved into the panels of the door is about the meeting at the temple between the beautiful Queen of Sheba and King Solomon. In this scene alone there are almost one hundred characters. The sculptor Lorenzo Ghiberti certainly wasn't lazy!

19

This animal is the symbol of the strength and simplicity of the Florentine Republic: the **Marzocco**. It's a lion made of gilded metal, and it's at the top of the palace tower.

Unwanted visitors had a 'warm welcome' dropped on them from these openings – boiling oil, for example, or stones!

The iron rings you can find all over the place inside and outside Palazzo Vecchio were used… to park the horses by tying them up by their halter.

The Florentines call it "il Biancone" – big whitey! It's Neptune, king of the sea, on top of his fountain in **Piazza della Signoria**.

It has this name because eventually it got… old. The Medici family, the overlords of the city, used to live here, but in the 16th century they decided to move house and went to live in a new palace called Palazzo Pitti. And so it became known as the 'old' palace. Anyway, with all those battlements and defences it was more like a fortress than a house. Originally it was called "Palazzo dei Priori", the priors being the governors of the city. They all lived together in the palace and hardly every left it. If one of them happened to go out for a stroll, they all had to go together! Florence is still governed from the rooms of this building.

Perseus has just cut off the head of the terrible Medusa, whose gaze turned people into stone. Beneath his feet is the headless corpse, with blood jetting out from the neck. The sculptor Benvenuto Cellini had big problems casting this bronze statue, which you can see in the **Loggia dei Lanzi** next to Palazzo Vecchio.

WITH THOSE WINGS ON YOUR FEET YOU OUGHT TO BE A COURIER!

Judith was really heroic as well. Her story is told in the Bible: she went alone and at night into the tent of the terrible tyrant Holofernes and killed him. This is Donatello's depiction of her. You'll find her in the **Sala dei Gigli**.

IT'S BETWEEN US TWO, HOLOFERNES!

The magnificent **Salone dei Cinquecento**. The lords of Florence had the walls of the room covered with enormous tapestries depicting important battles won by the Florentine armies.

Here you can see a victory over Siena. It was a rather unusual battle because it took place at night, which was very rare in those days. That's why some of the soldiers are carrying lanterns to see where they're going. Some of them are wearing a white tunic – that was always obligatory when fighting at night!

25

the children's museum

MuR Fi

Museo *Ragazzi* | Firenze

There's a children's museum in Palazzo Vecchio, but it's not only for children! It provides activities and services for children, adolescents and adults. There are five special-experience workshops, three secret passages, an encounter with a character from the 16th century and twelve multimedia stations where you can discover the secrets of the palace that once belonged to Cosimo I de'Medici.

'*The Magic of the Lens*' laboratory is devoted to the telescope invented by Galileo, with the modification of an optical toy made in the Low Countries. You can observe the main characteristics of light and see how various types of lenses function. You'll discover that our world is not formed by objects but by light images.

The laboratory also has an extra attraction... up on the roof. Up amidst the blackbirds you'll find reproductions of three different telescopes, which you can use to look at the cathedral dome as if through the eyes of Galileo and his contemporaries.

The Bia and Garcia games room is for the smallest children and it's named after two of the children of Cosimo I. Imagination, poetry and magic in a workshop where you can invent games and suggest experiences.

You can play in an island of light and colour. Make masks, disguises and musical instruments from recycled materials. Take part in a shadow or a puppet show telling the story of the prince and the poor man.

You can help the Grand Duke to dress up in fancy, complicated clothes. You can dress up as one of his children. And you can discover how they used to wrap up new-born babies and what toys children of your age used to use.

In the *'Clothes and Body'* workshop you can meet Grand Duke Cosimo I de'Medici, his wife Eleonora da Toledo and some of their children.

29

In the map room of Palazzo Vecchio, the 'wardrobe' with the map of Armenia hides a secret passage, and if you go along it, climbing some steep stairs, you come to the *'Palace Architecture'* workshop.

There are five special-experience workshops, three secret passages, an encounter with a character from the 16th century and twelve multimedia stations where you can discover the secrets of the palace that once belonged to Cosimo I de'Medici.

the bargello

Behind these windows there are some really beautiful works. Look, for example, at the owl on the opposite page.

EAT ME IF YOU CAN!

HA HA!

This small fortress was built for the 'captain of the people', who was called the "Bargello" and was a kind of police chief. In fact this fortified palace was used as a prison for centuries. But don't expect to find any cells, instruments of torture or gallows because they were all removed in the 18th century. Today it's a museum with sculptures, paintings, jewels, arms and ancient fabrics.

This **owl** was done by a sculptor called **Giambologna**. The idea was to use it to decorate a grotto in a garden fit for a prince, together with other bronze birds.
The great advantage was they didn't make a mess and never asked for food!

33

David, the young boy who knocked off Goliath with just a sling. It's made of bronze and was done by Donatello, who perhaps had a liking for stories where the weak proved stronger than the strong. David's foot is resting on the big mug of the dead Goliath.

The **helmet of the Bargello**, the police chief of those days. It's a highly decorated headpiece, but he mainly put it on for parades. It made him look important and warlike.

WHAT`S THAT?

TOMBS! RATTLE RATTLE!

The Medici Chapels behind the Church of San Lorenzo are basically special tombs for VIPs. They contain the spectacular tombs of the Medici. From outside you can see the domes – the one on the Chapel of the Princes looks a lot like the cathedral dome. The small dome at the bottom right was built by a great artist whose name was Michelangelo.

The characters lying around on the cover of this tomb are **Day** (the man) and **Night** (the woman). Together Day and Night symbolise the passing of time. They were done by Michelangelo.

The fresco in one of the little domes depicts… a date. In fact, the position of the stars precisely indicates the night of 16 July 1416, the day Piero de'Medici was born.

36

THAT'S THE CHURCH OF SAN MARCO!

HEY! THERE REALLY ARE ANGELS HERE!

In the Dominican convent of San Marco there are the works of a man who was both a painter and a monk. His name was Fra Giovanni da Fiesole, but he was also known as Beato Angelico, because the angels he painted were the most beautiful – and angelic – of them all.

He's said not to have painted for money but out of faith and because he liked decorating the house where he lived with frescos. That house, of course, was the convent.

The printing press didn't exist when Angelico was alive. All books were written and illustrated by hand, and were called **"illuminated codices"**. He painted this one.

Look how many shades of colour there are on the angel's wings! They're still bright and vibrant because the fresco technique allows the colours to sink into the wall and become part of the plaster.

the accademia

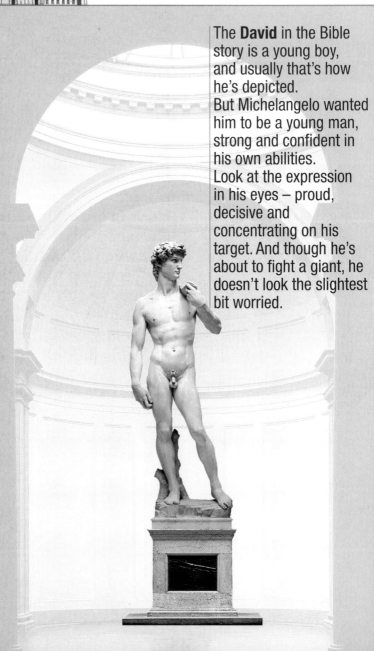

The **David** in the Bible story is a young boy, and usually that's how he's depicted. But Michelangelo wanted him to be a young man, strong and confident in his own abilities. Look at the expression in his eyes – proud, decisive and concentrating on his target. And though he's about to fight a giant, he doesn't look the slightest bit worried.

There's one work in this gallery that overshadows all the rest: Michelangelo's *David*. Everyone's familiar with it but why exactly is this statue so famous? What's the big deal? Well, its history for a start. It was sculpted from an enormously tall and narrow block of marble which no one dared use because it was full of defects – there was the risk it might break. But Michelangelo gave it a go, and what he had in mind was to depict David just as he's about to flatten Goliath. He finished it without problems in a record time of two years.

I'M DAVID, PLEASED TO MEET YOU!

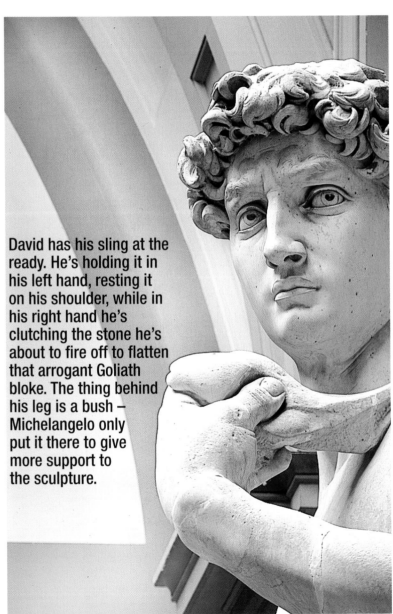

David has his sling at the ready. He's holding it in his left hand, resting it on his shoulder, while in his right hand he's clutching the stone he's about to fire off to flatten that arrogant Goliath bloke. The thing behind his leg is a bush – Michelangelo only put it there to give more support to the sculpture.

In actual fact **David** is himself a bit of a giant! Without his base on he's over four metres tall, and it took four days to move him in a cage – with the help of ropes and winches – from the artist's workshop to Piazza Signoria. And that's where he stayed till he was taken to the Accademia several centuries later, this time on a railway truck running on real tracks. Waiting for him was a specially-prepared room called the Tribune. His old place in the piazza was filled by a copy, which is still there. There's another one in Piazzale Michelangelo, so in all there are three David's!

David has also been attacked once. In 1991 a vandal went for his left foot with a hammer, and splintered it. The restorers 'made it better' by putting the fragments back in the right place.

There are other important guests in the **Accademia**, also done by Michelangelo. These are the prisoners (the work is called *I Prigioni*) and in fact the male figures look as if they're trapped in the marble and are making a massive effort to free themselves.

LET ME OUT!!

The work is actually unfinished and from close up you can even see the marks of Michelangelo's chisel. Thin and criss-crossed on the more finished surfaces, deeper and further apart where the marble has only been roughly worked. But the struggle of these mysterious characters to escape from the unformed material is so powerful and expressive that the statues don't look unfinished at all.

These ceramic babies, which are all wrapped up (no nappies in those days!), were basically a hospital sign and clearly indicated that it was an orphanage. But they're works of art too!

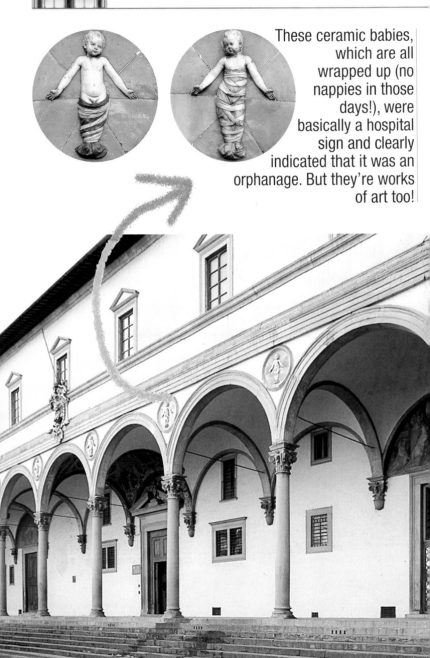

There's a very important Renaissance building in the piazza: the Spedale degli Innocenti, the hospital of the innocents. There was a small revolving door under the portico where it was possible, day and night, to leave unwanted new-born babies instead of abandoning them in the streets or the woods as often happened. Wet nurses and tutors would then take care of these small innocents, hence the name of the building. When they grew up, the children were taught various professions so they could earn a living. The city tried to look after its children, even the least fortunate ones.

In the piazza there are two identical fountains. They look like two large bronze shells in which pairs of little sea beasts spit water for evermore. They were made for the port of Livorno but they turned out so well that the Florentines decided to keep them for themselves.

Indiana Jones would like this museum, because it's full of fabulous finds from the ancient past. Here you can find objects from Etruscan, Greek, Roman and Egyptian civilisations which tell us something about what our ancestors were like and how they lived.

There are, of course, incredible works of art as well.

PUSS, PUSS!

One of the most beautiful items is the **Etruscan Chimera**. Made of bronze, it's a terrifying beast, a cross between a lion, a goat and a snake. The story is that it used to spurt flames from its jaws. Defeating it was easier said than done! But the hero Bellerofonte managed it by pushing a lead-tipped lance into the mouth of the beast. The heat of the fire in the beast's belly melted the lead and the chimera died of… indigestion.

This tiny house or temple is a funeral urn. It contained the ashes of a dead Etruscan. The dead were also buried in tombs of various shapes and sizes, which have survived till now because they were made of stone. Not much remains of the houses of the Etruscans because they were made of wood and other not very resistant materials.

The cover of an **Egyptian sarcophagus** that contained the mum-my of Cesraperet, the wet nurse of a pharaoh's daughter. Some make-up items – a jar of cosmetics and a mirror – were found together with the mummy.

"Opificio" means laboratory. In this rather special laboratory stones such as lapis lazuli and agate were crafted into all sorts of objects: table surfaces, wall and floor panels, and even pictures. These works was done so perfectly and were so well-known that this extremely difficult technique is still called 'Florentine mosaic'. Nowadays the Opificio mainly does restoration work but in the museum you can see old works, preparatory designs and the instruments they used.

A piece of **inlay** isn't a mosaic. In a mosaic you can see the lime between one tessera and another, while here there's no space between the stones because of the incredible skill and patience of the artists. Of course the stones are fixed with an adhesive, which is hidden underneath. Some of these stones came from a long way away (Asia, the Americas), while others were taken (as was the custom in those times) from the ruins of ancient Rome.

What you can see here isn't a painting, it's a puzzle of semi-precious stones, an **inlay**. Every tiny little part of it is a small piece of stone carefully cut so it fits perfectly with the piece next to it. The colours and shades are given by the natural hues and veining of each stone. The result is a smooth, shiny and very colourful surface, exactly as it was when it was first made. It's so unchangeable that some people call it 'eternal painting'.

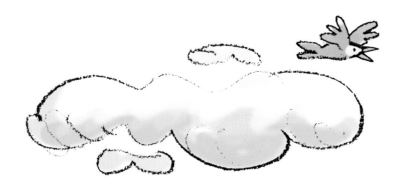

boboli gardens

The Medici family were so proud of their parks that they had them painted by a Flemish artist in lots of moon-shaped paintings known as lunettes. This one is of the Boboli Gardens as they were five centuries ago. Italian princes thought a garden ought to be a kind of natural 'extension' to the house. An open-air living room where instead of furniture there were trees and hedges cut into geometrical patterns. Not to mention fountains, aquatic devices and artificial grottoes. That's how the famous 'Italian garden' came into being.

For hundreds of years now this **Neptune** has been on the point of hurling his trident into the water of a pool where they once used to rear fish for court banquets.

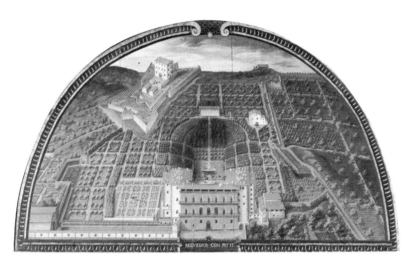

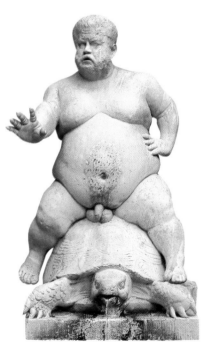

The fat guy sitting on the turtle really existed. His name was **Morgante** and he was the most well-known and favourite dwarf at the Medici court. He looks like a bit of a joker!

The small lake at the end of the row of cypresses is called the "**Vasca dell'Isola**" – the island pool. Lemon plants are placed on the centre of the island in the summer, but in the winter these delicate plants keep themselves warm in "limonaie", which are specially-designed greenhouses built by the gardeners at Boboli.

The artists of the time reckoned they could do better than nature, and designed the gardens so the vegetation didn't grow any old how but according to very regular patterns. Sometimes, as in this case, they also created seemingly natural grottoes decorated with statues and fake rocks. **Bernardo Buontalenti** was something of an expert at them.

Forte Belvedere at the top of the hill of Boboli was a bolt-hole for the Grand Dukes in case of danger. They also kept their treasure here in a special thief-proof room.

In fact any would-be thief would have had to deal with a drawbridge, a device with harquebuses that fired if you tried to force the security doors, a trapdoor that fell open onto a well filled with sharpened stakes, and a millstone crashing down from above. If that didn't do the trick there was a way of flooding the room completely to ensure it was curtains for the thief. Scrooge was nothing compared to this!

Part of the secret corridor linking Palazzo Vecchio and Palazzo Pitti. It's said that there was always a carriage ready and waiting at the exit to rush the prince off to his refuge in Forte Belvedere.

THE BOBOLI
GARDENS BELONGS
TO THIS PALACE!

palazzo pitti

IT`S PALAZZO
PITTI!
NOT A BAD
LITTLE PLACE!

The Palatine Gallery, the Silverware Museum and the Carriage Museum are all in Palazzo Pitti, home to the rulers of Florence from the 16th century onwards. During court feasts, one favourite game was playing... naval battles. The courtyard would be filled with water and then carts disguised as ships would board and sink each other. Sounds like good fun, doesn't it?

The **Medici** family collected art works but also jewellery and other precious objects. They used to ask the artists of the time to make things to add to the family collection. Most of them are now kept here.

This round painting is a Madonna with Child together with a young St John. It was done by **Raphael** and is exhibited in a room once known as the "quadreria" – the picture room. The Medici used to hang their favourite pictures here and not much has changed since they were around.

In 19th century Tuscany there was a group of artists who defined themselves as "**macchiaioli**". They painted everyday things with blobs of paint ("macchie") and with sharp contrasts between light and shade. Here's one example – *La Rotonda di Palmieri* by **Giovanni Fattori**.

This child looks like he has the makings of a good sculptor! In actual fact not only did he do well as a sculptor, but he was also a painter, writer and architect. This is **Michelangelo**, one of the greatest geniuses ever.

The Costume Museum in **Palazzo Pitti** has a collection of clothes, shoes, hats and other things from the past. It gives you an idea of how both young and old dressed all those centuries ago. Things have changed a bit since then, haven't they?

The Silverware Museum contains almost all the precious objects collected by the various members of the **Medici** family. They tended to start their own personal collections while also trying to add to those of their fathers and grandfathers. It was something of a family tradition!

On the right-hand side of the Palazzo Pitti facade, in the so-called Rondò, is the entrance to a rather unusual museum. In it are seven carriages that belonged first to the Medici-Lorraine Grand-Dukes and then to the Savoy family. They all ruled Florence at one time or another. Basically this was the garage of the rich and powerful. There's also old harness and tackle for horses, and a pair of sedan chairs.

MINE'S SIX HORSEPOWER! AND YOURS?

This carriage is the super luxury model. It's entirely covered with gold plate and was pulled by six horses. Only a prince could afford something like this and it's what nowadays would be called a status-symbol.

WALK?
GULP!

If you look at the top you can see the **prince's corridor**. In order to go to work in the morning and get on with the job of governing Florence, Grand Duke **Cosimo I** had to cross the river Arno, but as he didn't want to mix with the crowds, he got the architect **Vasari** to build a private pathway from his home to the office.

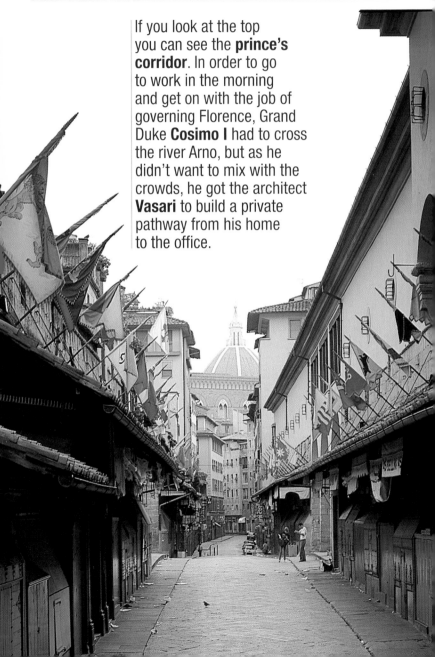

WHAT
A STINK!

It's one of the strangest bridges in the world. It's like going along any old street, and it's only when you're halfway across that you realise you're suspended over the river Arno. That's because of all the shops lining both sides, those little houses that you can see 'hanging' on the piers of the bridge. In the past they were butchers' shops, but fridges didn't exist then and the smell of rotting meat was sickening. Grand Duke Cosimo I crossed the bridge every day using a special corridor above the shops, and as he had a delicate nose he got rid of the butchers and had them replaced with the city's goldsmiths, who are still there today. Gold doesn't smell!

In this photo you can clearly see the point where the **Vasari Corridor** joins the **Uffizi**.

The route of the Vasari Corridor from **Palazzo Pitti** to **Palazzo Vecchio** .

In order to take the corridor across the **Ponte Vecchio**, Vasari had to take it round a tower at the head of the bridge, because the family who owned it wouldn't give permission for the corridor to go through it. The Grand Duke wasn't so powerful after all!

Nowadays there's a great gallery of self-portraits by famous painters in the **Vasari Corridor**. The collection is continually being added to with new works.

From the 'portholes' in the corridor there's a rather unique view of Florence. If you want you can take a walk along the corridor, but you have to book first.

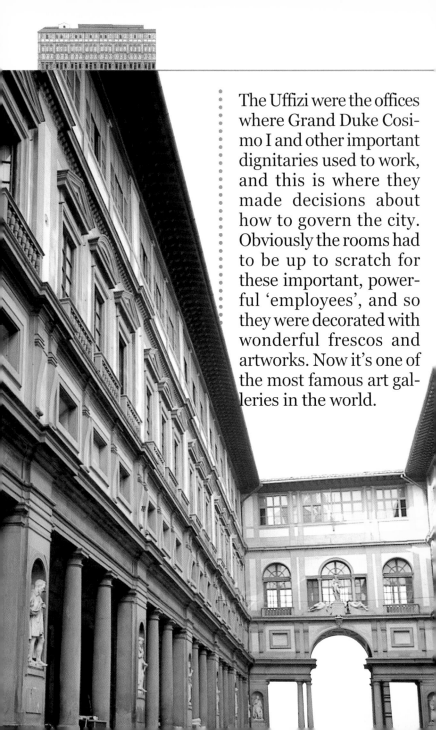

The Uffizi were the offices where Grand Duke Cosimo I and other important dignitaries used to work, and this is where they made decisions about how to govern the city. Obviously the rooms had to be up to scratch for these important, powerful 'employees', and so they were decorated with wonderful frescos and artworks. Now it's one of the most famous art galleries in the world.

Botticelli's Venus
just born from out of the
sea spray. By the looks
of her, she won't
be needing a baby
bottle – the gods were
born grown-up. This
painting (there's just one
detail here) is the oldest
existing canvas. Before
that they used to paint on
wooden panels. The
luminous, delicate colours
are the result of using a
'thin' tempera mixture
without adding any…
egg. In fact egg yoke was
often used at that time to
make the pigments of the
various colours denser.

DO I LOOK
LIKE HER?

79

This painting by Sandro Botticelli represents **Spring** and belonged to no other than Lorenzo il Magnifico.
Who are all these characters? The young woman on the right being chased by the flying man is the nymph Chloris. That's strange – there are flowers coming out of her mouth! The young guy with the long hair and a blue cloak is the wind Zephyr, who's in love with Chloris. And the woman dressed in flowers? She may be Spring, scattering flowers on the ground around her feet.

This little musical angel is small enough to fit into your backpack, but it might have been 'cut out' from a much larger work, perhaps a painted altar-piece.

WHAT ABOUT ME?

Psiche (with the butterfly's wings) is in love with Love personified (the one with the bird's wings). But Love was a flighty god and didn't want her to look at him. Psiche didn't obey him and Love disappeared. She didn't give up though. She found him again, was forgiven, and they've never been apart since.

This round painting is one of the most important paintings in the gallery and is known as the *Doni tondo*. It was done by Michelangelo, who evidently wasn't satisfied with sculpting figures but liked painting them too.

There's no doubt it's very beautiful, and Michelangelo, who had to sell it to the person who'd commissioned it, Angelo Doni, asked for the very high price of seventy scudi. Doni said he was willing to pay him forty but no more, whereupon Michelangelo proudly replied that in the meantime the price had gone up and if he still wanted it, it would cost a hundred! When they'd finished haggling, Michelangelo's pride had got the better of Angelo Doni's caution, and he had to hand over one hundred and forty scudi for the painting he loved.

This terrifying **Medusa**, with snakes instead of hair, was painted by **Caravaggio** on a **tondo** which had a rather particular use: it was a battle shield. According to the myth, the gaze of Medusa turned any enemy who dared look her in the eyes into stone.

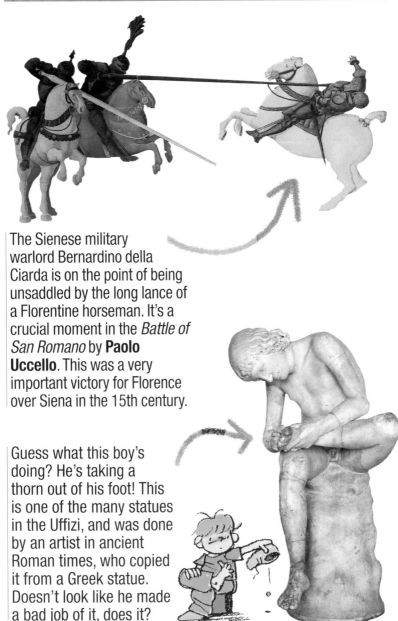

The Sienese military warlord Bernardino della Ciarda is on the point of being unsaddled by the long lance of a Florentine horseman. It's a crucial moment in the *Battle of San Romano* by **Paolo Uccello**. This was a very important victory for Florence over Siena in the 15th century.

Guess what this boy's doing? He's taking a thorn out of his foot! This is one of the many statues in the Uffizi, and was done by an artist in ancient Roman times, who copied it from a Greek statue. Doesn't look like he made a bad job of it, does it?

palazzo davanzati

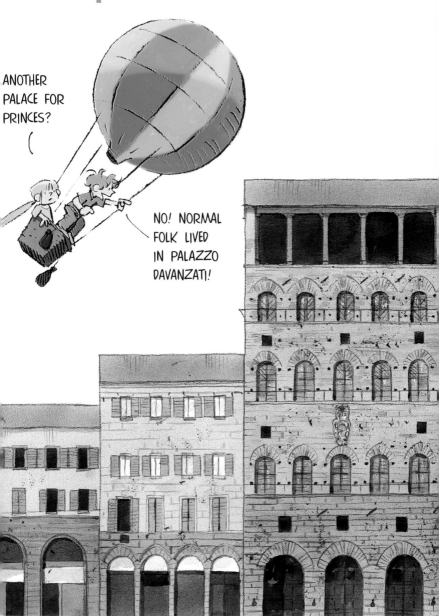

 palazzo davanzati

85

Palazzo Davanzati wasn't the house of kings, queens or princes but rather the family of a cloth merchant. Anyone visiting these rooms today can get a good idea of how normal people lived in the 14th century. To be sure, it was the house of a rich family, with luxuries that not many people could afford: a private well for drinking water, lamps, a fire place and servants to keep everything working.

But compared to today, even the richest of the rich had a pretty uncomfortable life.

A loggia for hanging out and drying cloth.

This room is decorated with frescos imitating curtains hanging on the walls. Covering the walls with heavy hangings was a way of keeping the heat in. In winter rooms that didn't have a fireplace were very cold, and a wool cap was an absolute must day and night!

What a great bed. The canopy was there to provide protection against draughts and against insects falling off the ceiling. If it was very cold they could draw the curtains so the bed was much warmer and more comfortable.

87

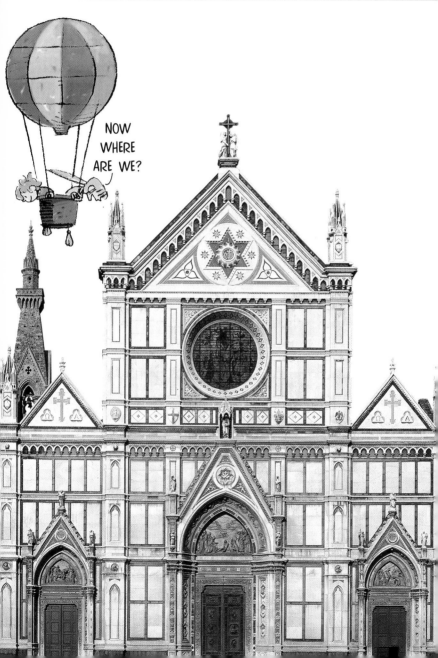

In ancient times the large piazza in front of the church was used for fairs and markets, jousting and tournaments, and also for playing football. But that's not all: large crowds often gathered to listen to the sermons of the Franciscan monks. So all these people could also listen to the word of God under the protection of a roof, the monks built the Basilica of Santa Croce. That's why it's so big – almost as big as the piazza.

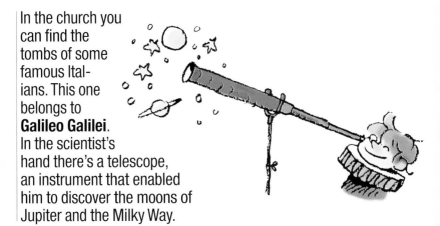

In the church you can find the tombs of some famous Italians. This one belongs to **Galileo Galilei**. In the scientist's hand there's a telescope, an instrument that enabled him to discover the moons of Jupiter and the Milky Way.

89

Despite the damage, **Cimabue's** *Crucifix* is still an extraordinary piece of work. It's had a rough time of it – in 1966 the river Arno broke its banks and flooded Florence, and the crucifix was covered by four metres of mud and water which removed large areas of paint. The Florentine restoration experts hunted round in the mess for the tiny fragments of the painting and patiently put them back into place. It was a bit like doing the most difficult puzzle in the world!

Frederick Stibbert was a Florentine who was crazy about old arms and armour. He collected so much of it that he filled the villa where he lived. Today it's a unique and fascinating museum with thousands of swords, lances, harquebuses and armour of all kinds.

Horse armour was used a lot until the 15th century, but then the invention of harquebuses and firearms made them useless because the bullets could pierce them.

Here you can see a Japanese helmet and battle mask. Part of the trick was to frighten the enemy!

Children didn't fight in wars, but they could take part in parades, where they wore armour like this. There were two problems with armour: it weighed a lot and it cost a lot. Only knights and cavaliers from rich families could afford it. Come to that, horses and equerries were pretty pricey as well!

There's room for all kinds of arms in **Mr Stibbert's** collection. Look at this pistol: you can see the whole working mechanism.

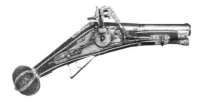

93

LOOK OUT!
THE BALLOON'S
FLAT!